BULLDOZER

David Alvarez
Cape Town, VI 12004

By the same author:
WAITING FOR LEILA

BULLDOZER

Achmat Dangor

RAVAN PRESS   JOHANNESBURG

Published by Ravan Press (Pty) Ltd
P.O. Box 31134, Braamfontein, 2017

First published 1983

ISBN 0 86975 144 1

Typesetting: Ginah Dludla
Cover portrait: Mpikayipheli Figlan
Cover design: The Graphic Equalizer
Printed by Blackshaws (Pty) Ltd, Cape Town

For 'J' and 'B'

CONTENTS

SHEILA'S DAY

She leaned against me
the servant girl
and then quietly
let her dress fall
with the calmness
of the sea against
the harbour wall

then she went away
to the Joburg
in Doornfontein
acquired a house
a man, and a child
with eyes as blue
as the sea
Sies!

THE COLOUR OF LOVE

Light a candle, love
one candle is enough
to reveal in the half-darkness
who we are
and where we are

Look: how the darkness
of our bodies dances
on the darkness
of the walls,
the flame subsides
and stands rigidly erect

How dark are your eyes
the darkness of the earth,
how red the flame of your lips
the red of the Karoo

Dark is the fruit of our desire
ripe as the colour of a wound,
blow out the candle, love,
in that brief moment
I see drops of sweat,
black pearls
on a masked face.

PARADISE

Oh paradise,
cool paradise of Africa
your sea roars
like the restless roots
of our lives

and yet does not give life
to the dreams
of the people
you have forgotten.

Here, around me,
they destroy my city.
District Six,
they dismantle you
— stone by stone —
rock of my history.

On the walls
of my last refuge
cockroaches run
secretive and quiet,
an omen:
love and hope
that will have to
be hidden in darkness.

Somewhere in the twilight
a banjo trills, somewhere
on an overgrown terrace
people sing and people laugh,
the human voices of everyday.

Oh paradise, cool paradise
of Africa,
what memories you recreate.

Oh why, why do you
tighten the chains?

MY AFRICA

This is my Africa:
the earth trembles
the heart beats
far from the savannahs
crowned with gold

Here in the cities
the trains hurtle
across crumbling bridges
(gunfire in the streets)
across the swirling waters
(screams)
at the speed of death
(a bitter quiet ensues)

Oh Mother
your pastoral dream
is dead
(Soweto burns)
is buried
without ash or earth

When shall the lanterns
hissing and stirring
to the rhythm
of our songs
again shine
in the windows
of grief?

VOICES ACROSS THE RIVER
(New Brighton, Port Elizabeth)

Do you hear those strident
voices across the river?
(and the river is of gold
the dappled waves fall
lap, lap,
like the slatternly fall
of the aia's dress)
oh listen to the voices
rise with the squall.

There are lights
in the windows of squalor,
and dancing in the streets,
their song rises through the fog,
it's the carnival of light.

Oh that I am a man
and cannot hold
the light gathering
in my eyes.

TUIS

My friend,
smile if you wish,
they praise you
because you are young
and you're black,
you are fire and mystery,
hotblooded and redblooded,
blooded upon the same
whetting-stone as I.

When we crawl back
to this sanctuary,
and pocket our frantic claws
(furtively, when the streets are empty)
we'll enter with a calm
and measured knock.

She will shrug and say:
'Ja-nee. Jy's tuis nê.'

AN EXILE'S FAREWELL

They talk of grief
as if it were
a flower
that the dead carry
to enhance their departure.

I can think only of you:
skin stretched taut,
dour parchment,
matted hair
that tangled in my hands,
your subterranean river
lapping faintly
in my ear.

You did not dance
in the flaming day
before their flickering eyes;
they found their flower
in Bethlehem,
for you hid your virtue well.

I take with me no memory,
no thought, no taste,
sufficient:
a quiet farewell,
Lieberstein and sour bread,
before your simple house.

AN EXILE'S LETTER HOME

I remember where I am
sitting
on cold cobblestone,
this is not home.

I cannot forget
where I am not,
for I remember
the place you built
for me,
on the banks
of Swartkopsrivier,
whose breezes blow
stolen words to me.

Dear Sir,
have they forgotten me?
Have they built for me
no monuments
at Slagtersnek
or Hoenderkop
or Kafferskraal

Dear Sir,
I cannot forget
why I am here.

A NOTE ON PATRIOTISM

The leech loves the land
during the flowing harvest time,
praises,
(and bitterly appraises)
neighbourly pastures
when the hungry hours come . . .

patriots march with faith
holding their flags like wreaths

oh come, flowing harvests,
come, for the good of your land!

THOSE WHO DO NOT SLEEP

Your shadow falls
upon my waking day,
and because you cannot
pull them out from
the frozen ground,
you stand on my roots
until they hurt

Yet together now
we shuffle in
the cold out here,
our heads loll
as we grow old
by the graves of our land

and in the dark
we splash about,
one eye forever open

while those who sleep
do not care,
even for the careless yawns
they throw in the street

where still the shadow
meets the sun unequally
on both our halves.

SCORN

They stopped us
outside the station,
'Where's your pass?
And you? Portuguese?
O! Malayer hê?
God. With a kaffir girl.'

I held you then,
Dear Ina, dear Ina,
flower of the night
wilting in the merciless light.

THE LADY ON THE BALCONY

Adriana van Stratus
lower your eyes
to the man waiting
in the black shadows
of this heat,
hair blowing
in the wind

but he is white
and she coloured

and words find their order,
fall neatly into slots.

SUMMER

Summer comes with
restless winds,
blows flowers about
in the city stalls.
Come, let us go, let us go,
there's a storm coming!
And summer passes
with a sigh.

The wind blows
above the corn,
there's a storm coming,
reap! reap!
or the corn will die.
And the wind howls
across the empty earth,
dust upon the windowsills.

The storm comes
from the North,
the tides are high,
sailors will die
upon the rocks tonight,
listen, the wind lurks
dust-laden in the hills.
Are the sheep penned,
the cattle in the kraal?
Lord, Lord, will we be able
to get out at all?

THIS WAS SUMMER
(taken from the journal of a prematurely retired whore)

'I showed him
the Botanical Gardens
quiet bars
the cable way
when I took him
to my room
in Hanover street
he said
Your City's Got Life

he spoke furtively
to the man
in the goatee beard
(how does he hide the dagga
on that skeleton frame)
Chinese suyi
American whiskey
that class of man.
This was summer

until I found him beside
the girl who hid her lemon buds
with trembling hands,
his smile told me
I did not understand

a virgin in braided plaits
has every right,
he gave me a medallion
MADE IN HONG KONG.
Baby, the summer's over.
I still did not understand.'

COMMUNION
*(In celebration of Shaka's birth,
if he were born today)*

I
This madness came to me
with breezes from the Karoo,
strewing pollen about the air

And I am germinated,
full upon this holy river
and the river is in flood

taking lilies
and other unexotic buds
dead flowers
to their burial by the sea.

II
Oh men of the earth,
rats at the door of heaven,
I bloom,

not the blooming of corn
or the greening
of dull pastures
where gods of men are born

I sing my song
among these craggy rocks
where the wind
is not companionable

I bloom black as the night
from hole to hole.

JOURNEY THROUGH A NAKED LAND

I
Solitary Sunday spires:
'God flourishes
in this arid land,
white collars
black suits
burning in the sun.

Beaufort
blaukrantz
the amethyst hills beyond
tattered rags clothe
wine-red eyes,
three hundred years
of lineal shame
sternly dressed
in immaculate Afrikaans,
from row upon row
of vegetable hovels
expired breath
blows hotly
to the turbulent sea.

Silence in a rattling taxi
Home Please.
Where's Home, Master?
behind the mist
of a weeping eye.

II
In the vineyards
broken fingers grow
stumps that smoothe

the wrinkled folds
on faded whores,
musty odours
cling carnally:
red dust in a parched throat,
pale eyes droop off to sleep
tired,
tired of growing old.

The grass waves
in drunken somnambulance
beside the grave
of the besotten beggar
who exposed the vivid veins
of his enormous sex
to her virgin eyes
(the master hung him
from the neck of his tree)
swollen fruit
succumbs unsated
— one by rotting one —
to its own excessive sweetness
and falls stealthily
to the ground.

III
I ran beneath
the stooping bows
unclothed, unarmed
except for the naked eye
I do not know the valleys
I do not know the vineyard
mine is the naked land
where cold fingers
thumb the rigid leaf

word upon writhing word
silence sinks
heavily to the ground.

IV
The virgin lies
with aching thighs,
beside the beggar grave
the fruit drops
plip plop
to the maggots creeping
in my guts

that bitch shall
not lure me back
to her sordid bed
however green the earth.

V
And in the end
it ends with a knock
on the door,
I am home
to the hovel
of my birth
brother, share
with me
the warmth
of your stinking blanket,
the pleasures
of your sister whore

share with me
the breath of
your naked life.

SWANSONG
(Grahamstown 1978)

I
The old world decayed
like forgotten manners
in those great white houses,
polished cutlery,
sweet red wine,
servants ran to
call of bells,
bells wielded like whips,
bells that cracked
and did not peal.

Here I first saw you
in the midst of
all those lovelies
flying the great steps
of Rhodes,
wind and mayhem
in your thighs;
my ear, forever cocked,
awaited that Pretorian growl:
'Jy's 'n lawwe Boesman nê.'

For I come from
the naked land
whose austere hospitality offers:
'Hier's jou stukkie brood,
nou fok off.'
· And I go
curled up
in a corner of my world
to quell

the hunger in my heart.

II
In these pockets of silence
Fingo Village
the Coloured Quarters
the dusty breeze unpacks
the daily carnage
of my kind,
here you offered me
your lithe white body.
Look!
the hunger's not in my loins,
it's in my heart.

Beyond the circle
of our darkness
little black boys
in shiny serge sang
IN THE PROMISED LAND,
a tear gathered
in your eye.

I stayed behind
and drank the wine
watched Eliot and Voltaire
climb helter-skelter
up your wall
Genoeg!
it's time to say
goodbye.

III
Listen,
do you hear

the wind ransack
the open plains
of my heart,
do you hear
the crack of that bell?

Totsiens, farewell,
sien jou weer.

DURBAN 1973

Bluebottles
infested slagrock
too smooth too
slick for the sea's wild hand
waves lurched on shattered feet
seaweed oil broken glass,
and they marched
to the sea and back
rigidly holding hands.

I could not love you then,
the bony tourist
achaar bristling in
his stooping moustache
touched you
with his leprous smile.

STEYTLER STREET, NEWCLARE

There's no grass that's green
and nothing's cool

no churches
for nothing's good
nothing's bad
no fountain here
nothing's young
nothing's old

there's no sky
nothing's high
nothing's low
no vice
no virtue
in Christ's unjourneyed land.

THE GREY PEOPLE
(sketches of a squatter colony)

I

How can I weep for
the black loneliness
you unwrap from your eyes
and coil around my neck,
garlands for the living dead?
Come, we are here to bury him.
Living was not his business.

Kalie was a miner
who dug your body for gold
and hung there in the darkness
weeping for the maiden
left in Oranjeland,
dreaming the dreams
of forgotten men,
for whom virgins never wait.

II

Here are the remains
of his abandoned memories
scattered about your
pale fire.
His wine was good
until he sipped Meths
on your 'Bloutrein Express',
and journeyed, out of breath
to this derailment
in your spindly arms.

Come let us bury him
beneath the khakibos

where other whores have
hidden their seedy wares.
Look, the colour of vomit
sticks resolutely to his face.

III
Oh tend your broken fire
that cannot mend the world
which lost its way
behind your wall

who am I to judge,
who am I
not to love you
because you live
in the whorehouse
of the world?

THE HOUSE OF KING KALIE

I dream of coming home
to the twisting vine
that gnarls your dusty house,
where 'Dems and Dose'
stumble out,
those drunken urchins
with vengeful hands
that drag me from
my morose sleep
and shear my soiled
brown locks.

I stray along
the abandoned streets
of your sorry history
without my ancestor's
bastard pride,
and dream
of coming home.

JOURNEY TO THE FEAST OF SPRING

Have Pass. Can Travel.
He took a train
from Troy to Ithaca,
tin cans rattling,
blankets burdening,
stuffed his ears
from the cry of the cattle
at the slaughter house.
Died in his sleep
on a wooden bench.

I
The 5.41 does not arrive,
and the hope of my land
slide their hearts
into hidden pockets,
hang from open doors
draped like flags
on festival days.

We talked awhile
under the shuttered awning
will they nail him
to the cross
or send him into exile,
ice-cream vendors
ticket sellers
caught in the sun,
'Hey porter, porter,
here's a Black Boy
jus' fell down an' died,'
and stepped off at dawn

across an Afrikaner farm.
He wears his hat wide
and feeds a crippled dog
from a lame hand,
lives in rich constraint
off a withered land.
In gloomy storerooms
he collects his dusty wealth
in polished stacks,
and will not give
and will not take
from the shadowy light
creeping to his door.

II
It is time the rains came,
it is time to slaughter
a cow for the feast of spring
that is swept in dust
to a sparse end
by the pool of blood
on his stone.

It is time to till,
to march up
the great north road.
Have Pass. Can Dig.
It is time to reap,
to turn the stone again.

The music falls
in melancholy thuds
through the empty hours
when the vapid dreams
of little kings flee,

I shall hear
and not see,
touch and not feel
the mielie stricken
in the fields.

Where do my people
carry their hearts?

III
Welcome Home.
Eat.
Eat of the jackfruit
from your father's tree,
silence:
let no dumb mouth speak words
that cannot rid itself
of bitter tastes,
your father died of it.

Eat.
Eat of the leavened bread,
sadness is not
the black child's wine,
ancestral kisses
did not leave untouched
the visceral dream,
and cool water oozes
from the secret calabash.
Ebony smiles quiver
behind his back,
where sombre eyes
gather his bloom
in the forbidden
garden of joy.

Eh! Already Judas sits
upon the tribal chair
in the kingdom
of little tin soldiers.
Have Pass. Can Live.
Have Pass. Can Die.

But listen
to the gospel
of the reedy wind
play in the leaves
the whisper
of an unspoken word
as dry as marrowless bone,
that could not muster
the thought of you
wrapped in the tear of my eye

from a rotting drum it fell
and slunk through slimy pools,
rippling teeth gnaw
at the edge of his memory
the disconsolate timbre
of your forgotten voice.

IV
It is spring.
And spring died
on the bloodstone
of a lame hand.

No fruit grows
on the baobab tree
here nothing is
immaculately conceived;

stricken wombs
and broken hands
squeeze the wine of man,
no flowers adorn
the ashes
of withered kings.

On the walled road
the white hens dance
the strut strut strut
of glee.
Vastrap! Vasbyt!
Have Pass. Can Wait.

Our virgin God
rages in their gloomy temples
where lapdogs lap
polished altars
and priests dance unfrocked
on dusty beams,
chanting lowly
their sonorous hymns.

V
Though they dip
bleeding fingers
into the folds
of his thought,
do not stand with
wet eyes at his door,
no bloodied hands guard
the cradle of dreams,
no thorns crown
his dishevelled head.

Leave him in abandon
to the savage graces
of his love,
already the beat
of the cowhide drum
drapes the night
in˙indolent arms.

VI
The white hens
play in the fields,
the blood of spring red
upon their deadened beaks,
we, ensconced in our latticed minds
have slept to death
behind darkened windows.

The wind rattles the shutters,
the sun licks its shadows,
an awakening hand
reaches into a hidden pocket.

VII
It is night
it is day
that slinks
outside my door,
it is the cry of the cattle,
the lowing of our seething sons,
it is the bokmakierie
the bomb ticking in their hearts,
it is the sound of rain
the cry of spring
it is the anthem of the dead

and over the radio
a lonely European voice
announces:
'In Africa today
another child was born.'

SONG OF THE LITTLE MEN

I
The wind howls,
it was always like this
in the august months,
with nothing to do
but drift through
dry gardens
picking fallen flowers
in the winding path.

II
Oh the hours are spent
for the gallant men
dying of asthmatic coughs
in cheap hotels,
the hours are spent
for the heroic men
who spread their
consumptive breaths
across the land.

> 'Daar's ñ hoender
> om die draai
> gecollar en getie,
> wat gaan die ander
> hoenders sê?
> Keer hom, keer hom,
> keer hom met sy
> nekkie omgedraai.'

III
History is the havoc of
unlikely loins commingled
in bastard forests,

'the fornication
of time, accident
and Jan van Riebeeck,'
the New Nationalists said
   'Daar kom die Alabama,
   die Alabama die kom
   oor die see,
   O,o, die riete kooi
   die riete kooi
is vir my gemaak
om daarop te slaap.'

IV
Zarathustra went abroad
in a burlesque hat
and flowers in his head
to the shipwrecked
   and the dead,
the price of the living
      too high

'A bleddy rand I pay
fo' my bleddy piecer bred,
then dis ding ou Dina
comes te burrow,
Dina ek likes jou nie,
waai net toe, waai!
Fokoff, I tells the
      bleddy ding.'

   Ou Dina se ding is vim,
   hoor hoe slaan die gomma,
   die gomma gomma gomma,
   die gomma va' ta' Sera.'

V
Come to me
3rd Class sojourners,
the price of life is high,
(beyond the stench of carbolic),
this jolting, this jagged lilt
uplifts your tattered souls,
what grandeur in your broken backs!

Ekskuus! Dis my stop, dis
Heita! Who's standing
the bleddy door toe?

And they say
the devil's among us,
the criers fly
through the streets
the sky is blue and cold,
shall it hold?
shall the hardy people hold?

VI
'Darling summer comes again
with its restless air,
the smell of coolness
in dark summer rooms

can we go again, on a trip
along the Garden Route,
through the little town
they call Pacaltsdorp

the little men marched past
in the afternoon sun
waving to the terrace

where we sipped that wine
THE BLOOD OF THE BULL
in the purpling shades
of a magnolia tree,
did you not love '
that nakedness?'

Whose nakedness in
the valley of nakedness,
(those strong black arms,
those coal-black eyes
that stared at your thighs)
whose nakedness
chilled your flesh?

VII
I long for your inviolable legs
spread out on the table now
where your lovers sit
in mordant council
upon deadened hands

oh the innocent hours spent
on those golden terraces,
the Tango, the Square,
that divinely perfumed air
(indigo and emerald)
held such promise for
our lilting names
— duBarry, Dupont, De Bruin —

how that sleek lady glided
through the shabby crowds
lolling with menacing indolence
by the gleaming cars

HONK! HONK! VOERT! EKSKUUS!

And the song echoed
in the shattered hall
washed in light from
the star-lit terraces,
dans Susanna, dans!

'O Susanna,
wie het jou gemaak?
Wie't jou soe mooi gemaak
dat ek vi' jou soe smaak?'

SUMMER IN SOWETO

It was summer again,
hot and dusty,
and the shebeens
were full

There was much talk
of revolution,
for this is the topic
of the moulting season

We heard conversations
of Fidel in the Sierra Maestra
of Ché and Neto and Mugabe

In the evening we departed
filled with beer
and unease
(the sun slinks away
like a rat into the darkness)

In the street
there was a hungry boy
with outstretched arms,
dust on his tattered sleeve,
and the emptiness
of murder in his eyes.

ASCENSION

We met again
after many years,
you were pure,
bright and eager

but there was something new
in the way you crossed your legs,
a hint of dark-fleshed freedom,
a waywardness in your stance.

And after many hours
we had nothing
to offer each other
except the pain of dead memories,
a suffering that no longer
satisfies my soul,

I left the perfumed air
of your cleanly washed body
and went to the whores
in the township.

Now:
look at my body
spilled like wine-blood
in the gutter

I see a scarlet memory
forming in your eyes,
'I loved a poet once,
but he went to pieces.'

As you turn away

you do not see
the scattered fragments
like bloodied stars
mark my way to the heavens.

DESPAIR

I am rich
and dine with the poor,
we burn incense sticks
to quiet the troubled air,
the disquieting talk

The motor workers are on strike
milk workers on strike
workers on strike
strike

In their unsated faces
I see their silent satisfaction,
they have seen my fear

Through the sepulchral air
I walk to my bed
and cover my head to pray
to God my conspirator
iconed to the wall

They are wrong!
They are wrong!

THE GUERILLA

The dust of the August winds
swirls through the night streets
of Riverlea:
the place they call 'Zombie-Town'.

To the casual observer
half asleep in his limousine
(perhaps he is a police spy
or a member of the underground,
or a drunk trying to sober up)
this night would hold
no more menace
than any other night in Zombie-Town

even though the clouds of dust glow,
in the dead of night
a dull and murderous red,
and the dogs, ceasing their invasion
of the dustbins, begin to howl,
like children in pain.

A door opens,
the flame of a candle
dances nakedly, pale and tender
upon the putrefied air
of dust and darkness,
and is hastily extinguished.

A man walks into the street,
the grief of unuttered farewells
still upon his lips,
one would have expected
a bigger man, much taller,

One would have expected
a leaner look,
hungrier eyes.

What is it that makes
this man, with thin legs
and scrawny arms
slink off into the night
to join the guerillas?

Is it the hatred,
is it the anger in his eyes?
One cannot see,
for the dust obscures all this,
and even erases from his memory
the stale warmth of his home.

Is it the recollection of hunger?
Or the icy dampness of cold ash
on the soles of his feet
as he pads through the shadows
of his own childhood
to comfort a screaming brother
afraid of the demons
creeping up through the floor
on which he sleeps?

Is it the sting of teargas
that besieges and scatters
our dreams,
or the indelible pain
of prison bars?
Or is it the inky, liquid flow
of piss down your thighs
as you learn to say

BAAS! BAAS!
out of fear?

As he hurries through the streets
that jar and twist like memories,
down hidden alleys,
through back passages
that gleam with mud and shit,
fecund with incongruous hope,
he knows, it is all these things
and none of these things,

it is hatred
and it is love,
it is the will of the hand
that tills the stony ground,
that sows darkness
as the seed of light,
hours, and years,
before the sun
will be born again.

OPPRESSION
(a visit to old Newclare)

The smell of burnt-out candles,
of ash in the stove,
of carnality,
of unwashed mouths
that kiss you
sweetly still.

But something
makes the stomach turn,
perhaps the rotting floors,
or yet another wasted walk
to the blackened windows

They
have chained my memory
to poverty.

ELEGY FOR A QUEEN
(Known as the 'Madam' in District Six)

I
I heard that they had discarded you,
flung your body into the street,
and when I returned
you were too weak
to open your arms
in greeting.

I saw in your eyes
wind and empty spaces,
wind and empty spaces.

In your last days
they turned you
into a filthy whore

but even your seducers
can find no joy
in the manner
of your debauch.

Soon they will exhaust
their grey-suited power,
and still not find
a suitable grave
for your memory.

I shall carry it with me,
crushed by its embrace!

II
When I held your body,

even after it had been washed clean
by the mists of the mountain,
I could not dispel
the smell of poverty.

Your history is an array
of armpit odours,
the dankness of dark alleys,
salt and sweat
and the reek of silence
in an unwashed mouth.

But soon you will lie
in the arms of a gentleman,
a rich man dressed in white,
or a white man himself,
and he too will stink
of your irrevocable death.

THE SILENCE OF THE ROCKS

Oh my earth,
I have come to terms
with you.
I no longer sow
the seeds of my youth
in your womb

It is not
that my youth is gone
but your womb
is no longer a place
for youthful dreams
to grow

And all that falls
from the sky
onto your barrenness
are tears,
and whispers
of fear and pain

Once,
in the rain-filled mornings
of our love
we heard the seeds burst
and stir the roots of our lives

Now the hard and
poisonous bushes that grow
take nothing from
the light of day
except the deadly life
that it gives,

clutches to its bosom
the photosynthesis
of doom

The wind laments
that I no longer
sing with the
lyrical voice of the poet,
that my tongue
has become as hard
and sharp
as the silence
of the rocks

Let the wind, then, too
go into the ghettoes
of my kind,
and listen to the silence
as hard and sharp
as the silence of the rocks.

THE VOICES THAT ARE DEAD

I
There is a silence
upon the river tonight.
No great floods of song
flow out into the darkness,
our voices are dead.

And the midnight moon,
white and cold
over the ashen streets
reveals nothing but shadows
fleeing from one darkness
to the next.

Mattera, Mohapi, Mathe,
Nortje, Nakasa
and you Brutus,
names and voices
that few remember.

II
Oh, my brothers,
poets of the earth
who ripped handfuls
of flesh from the land
as salt for the tears
in your songs

And today,
like black madrigals
sing with gilded voices
in the great white halls,
at the soirées

of a people whose souls
are famished.

And you are their final
sad repast with
whom they sit down to sup
with the now uncertain air
of imperial ceremony.

Oh, my brothers —
you too are dead,
your voices rage barrenly
within the august halls
of the doomed,

but are not heard
by the cowherd who treads
his unknowing peace,
nor is it heard
in the ashen townships
where soon your memory
will flit unlovingly
from one darkness to the next.

III
Yet, I can write of hope,
though the voice I hear
in the icy dawn
is still frail and tremulous,
and the mists are a portend
of a familiar and savage storm.

I can sing a hymn
to the glory of my land,
from the ashes something stirs,

new voices are being heard.

I can look with love
at the harsh landscape
pockmarked by ghettoes.
In the dust and the dirt
new voices sing new songs.

Yet still the morning rises
as if drenched in blood.
Oh Lord, save them
from the gunfire
and the jackboot.

ONCE THERE WAS A POEM

These bitter words
tumble from me
like a flood

Do not wonder at this:
you it was who
milked the udders
of my love,
and left me nothing
but the venomous
dredges of despair

Come,
search the emptiness
of my heart,
and ignite
the dry tinder
of its substance,
and say:
Once there was
a poem here.

WE DRANK WINE TOGETHER

We drank wine together,
the sweet red blood
of our brothers
crushed from the
swollen testicles
of their lives.
Theirs is the slavery of love.

And through the luminous haze
oh taste of the sun!
oh taste of warm flesh!
I could see only
the twisted body of a young boy
— in a vineyard green
and heavy with rain —
crushed against the icy earth
for warmth.

I could not love you.
A child lay dead,
I tasted his death
on your lips.

MY NEW COMPANION

I have a new companion now,
she comes only at night
and climbs straight into bed,
she locks her arms around my soul,
and presses her knees into my brain
my new companion
has the thighs of a whore.

She is late tonight;
her face sleeps
in the shroud
of a filthy beard.

The mind of my sleep
withers under the eye
of a hungry ghoul,
my new companion
has the voice
of a love-hungry cat,
she calls,
I will not go.

With pouted lips
she kisses
tears from my swollen eye,
wraps its salt
around her tongue
and spits it out,
indifferently,
indifferently now.

she clucks her tongue
in a bitter mouth,

I had better go
my new companion
has a murderer's hands.

She records her life
in the diaries
of wrinkled men,
love is a burning body
pressed against frozen slabstone,
there was a time,
in all innocence,
when joy was a simple thing.

My new companion
has a mind
stuffed with flesh,
she begets her young
on rigid sheaves
of rotting leaves,
her thrashing legs
beat out bare tones
of loveless lives,
the Christs of late
are born with crowns of scorn,
their apostles
wear mitres of hate.

My new companion
has poisonous breasts.

She leaves her young
naked and cold,
her anger shatters
the opacity
of innocent windows,

climbs up
into sacred sanctuaries
and claws down the old gods,
any gods,
now there are none.
My new companion
has the instinct
of a beast.

She stalks the night
with hot, weary memories,
and when night falls,
takes its despair
and carves its skeleton
upon my heart.
She lies on her back
in a drunken stupor,
consumes my body,
and the night,
soon she will take
the dawn.
My new companion
has the appetite
of a pig.

I used to weep
fearfully in my sleep,
now I can flee,
a face in the mist
of faceless men,
drifting through
rainy nights,
there's something
about this summer
this age,

that I dislike
A scorched sun
drags its tired body
through choked ducts
of concrete arteries,
rimless eyes stare
at faded posters
in all-day cinemas,
somewhere in
the sea of heads
my new companion lurks.

BULLDOZER

Ja, ja
ons wiet vannie bulldozers
hulle kom oorie hiewel
wanne jy jou oege oep maak
(as jy jou bek oep maak
kry jy net stof innie keel)

en die vet ou jokkie
wat daar boege in sy
high seat sit en swiet
verlang net na sy
vris plaasmeisie
wat hy agter gelos het
om my pondokkie plat
te kom ry

en hy ry aan
oor anne hiewels
en anne pondokkies
anne liewens wa'
spat uit sy pad
en maa' weer wortels
êrens innie modder
laat sak

eendag
gaan die jokkie terug
na sy boeremeisie
oud van wag,
oud en gedaan
met die stof van
my gedane liewe.

BULLDOZER II

Hou op praat
vannie bulldozer
sy dag is veby
julle snaters onthou
net die sorry times

Wat vannie lekker tye
van eiers van
shilling a dozen,
vars melk vekoep
affie ou smous karre

En Abader se skreeu
(onthou jy hom nog?)
hoe jou oege gehang het
op die swaai van sy
jeugdige heupe

O liefie
treur jy nog
vir jou ou smous gubbe
'Melk! Melk! hiers' it
vars uitie koei
sikspens a pint!'

En agterna
sy ligte stap oppie trappe
'Is orraait, is orraait,
jou ou boy is nou net weg'
en liefde wat vloei
soes melk, vars uitie borste
vannie moederkoei.

BULLDOZER III

Nou loep os
op reguit paaie,
die wye bane
va ordentlikheid

Die is die winter
van os herinnering,
skraal is die wind
van os geskiedenis

Nee ou pellie
nie mee vir my
die warmte
vannie ou pondok,
hou jy maar
die broederskap
van armdom

Twaalf val die uur
oppie klok
met dieselfde geruk
vannie onskuldige kop
oppie butcherse blok

Kry jy die message ou pal?
Nie? Wel ek oek nie.
Wat vestaan os dom en stom
van die heavy psychology?
Man het mens geword
en hom hie kom plant
ry op ry in 'n
voorstedelike graf;
spook vannie twintigste eeu.

BULLDOZER IV

Hey ou pellie
jy's klaar nê?
dis al wat jy het
jou liewende karkas
is die pondok van jou siel
(kom klop die huisbaas nog
met krom hanne vir sy stuk rent?)
jy's uitgeput en uitgelief
'n squatter innie
squatterkamp van Tyd

Ennie bulldozer kom
ommie hiewel ou broe,
die laaste maal
jou huisie plat te ry,
hey waai man vegiet it
dust word dust, ashes en as,
jou liefde en jou liefling
'n gerimpelde ou knor,
wat staar jy soe velangend
na die son, wat hou jy soe vas?
fluit, fluit, jou storie is uit
wat hoep jy nog om te hope?

Kom saam met my, kom rus,
kom na die constellations toe.
Ek het daar vi jou
jou eie group area
'n huis en 'n tuin
ennie donkerwyn van ewigheid.
Het os nie altyd gesê
die Here ga' jou velos?

ODYSSEY

I
Doela was a Moor
from Kholvad
who defended his honour
in the hills
of Ahmedabad

and hid in the stink
of the Bay of Bombay
while the soldiers
of the British raj
those kwaai ouens
with the wax moustache

searched for him
in the heat of the day
(at night the moon hung limp)
beneath the fallen folds
of Indian girls,
until the fields
were red with their rape
'Doela, Doela gie op,
vi' onse sakes'

II
Doela sailed under
the Portuguese flag
Guam, Goa, Delagoa Bay,

Oemie, daars 'n Moor
by die deur
Wat wil hy hê?
Hy wil met Sathia trou

Sê die achaar-bek moet trap!

Maa' Doela en Sathia

('n regte child of rape)
en die kind van
'n slawevrou

Hy's té proud
hy dink hy's wonderful
hy dink hy's wie
en dink wie hy is

En Doela Moor
en Doela Moor se vrou
en Doela Moor se kind,
van Kholvad
en Ahmedabad
na Skotchieskloef
en Buitenkantstraat
dink wie hy is

Tien jaar op
Robbeneiland,
ons het hom gewarn,
jy kannie teen die
Government staan,
hulle is té powerful.
Junnie, dis histry nê?

DIE PATRIOT

Jy wiet mos hoe praat
julle altyds van ons
asof ons 'n blom
of iets of ander
groeisel uit die Karoo is

Daai 'salt of the earth'
klas van ding
wat jy oppie muur hang
wanne jy important vrienne kry

Maar ek belong, hoor jy,
al was ek oek
teen die muur gemaak,
uit die wrywing van
vleis en klip,
die issie land of my birth,
hoor jy?

Dissie joune nie,
dissie myne nie,
disse anne man se vrou
wat jy mee lol.

LEILA

Mustafa he' vir Leila gejol
met tamalytjiestroep
en chocolate joy
soe hand in hand
oorie Parara gestroll

Haar rok was wit
met 'n lace manel,
half price van ou Patel,
daar was soemer in haar oege

En Mustafa was jonk
(soe rare innie oorlog days)
en glad nie bad looking,
met sy gestriepte oenerbaaitjie
en sy Brylcream gladdies

Toe ry die drywer
sy City Bus
oor haar biene
'Kan jy nie kyk wa' loep jy?
Jou jintoe, het jy stof in jou oege?'

'Leila!'
Die wind en die meeue
versprei Mustafa se skreeu
'Leila!'
'Het jy stof in jou oege?'

POETRY

En nou staan hy en wag
Mustafa vir Leila
wie plat gery is
deur 'n City Bus

O! O! haar donke oege
haar olyf vel
my naam op haar lippe,
'n jintoe met
stof in haar oege
die hele poëtiese
idioom

Grys hang die meeue
soes winter blare
oorie dowwe see
en soe nou en dan
duik hulle af vir die
afvalkos van sy memry

wat lankal vegiet het
van haar geboorteplek
in Hanoverstraat
(van haar mank-oeg vader
in sy morsige oenerhemp)

wat net die wit rok onthou,
die wind innie lace manel
'Ons het oek 'n right om te love,
of hoe dan?'

DIE HELE STORIE

I
Vertel ons alles
die hele storie
hoe Adam en Eva
uit die hiemel
geval het

Jy wiet
hoe hulle oek
hulle liefde
moes wegstiek

Geskuilde glanse
die skelme voel-voel
oener die iet-tafel

Uiteindelik
in die skiemer
van soemer kamers
versadiging van
brandende lieste
(sweet tap jou af:
die heuning van verlange)

Dit was liefde jy wiet
heppie vir die liewe
wat heppie was
totdat die ou Derre
os oener os gatte skop

'Maggie God julle vegiewe
sukke lulike goede doen,
wel nie oner my dak nie.'

II
Sê dit soes it is
moe niks vestroep nie
vertel hoe my oupa
'n versotte Moses
(wie was 'n bietere slaaf?)
sy wandel eindig het

en af die slaafbote
uit die Jawa uit
sy kettings
hier kom sliep

vier jaar lank
het hy
die maan se silwer
kokorot graffiti
oppie kasteelmure
gelies

en toe kom sy Eva
na os Eden
haar half-chinees oege
en olyf vel
glinster innie
donker sel
en soe
tussen sug en giggel
met tronkvoël sekerheid
wassie saad gesaai

o soe was it gemaak, nê
met 'n giggel
die seun van man
uit die godelike beeld

(kommie geweldige lawaai)

III
Bly stil
julle robbishe
wat dink julle
die isse blerry hotel?
en wat stiek julle weg
kom laat os sien
laat os sien!
vir Gam vertrou
mens nie
vertrou die vertroubaar
die wat jy ken
die sweep en geweer
slot en grendel
slapende slawe
in 'n donker sel
maar in hierie stilte
groei die saad
vind skuiling
in donker hoekies
waar die gebibber
van eienaardige tonge
die son uitnooi
na 'n bloedige dood
en it roer
innie rooi
van die bloeiende oggend
dit isse tieken
die saviour kom
die seun van man

Haai sharrup
julle vuilgoed

72

dis noggie
Hotnot Krismis nie
wag tot Vrydagaand!

IV
Hiers iets annie brou
Kaptein, ek sê jou
ek voelit in my biene in
Ag wat worry jy soe
luister na my
ek is lank innie game in
'n slawekind
uit slawelieste
innie slawesel?
Ag jy worry veniet
hoorie, wat maakie nag
wat die donker
nie venietig?
dit spoel
oorblywende lig
van die dag
die gewete van man,
'n kers
in my donker nag.

V
Dit kom, die aand
sonder Magi
of aanduiende ster
in donkerte
en stilte
sonder erkenning
of ontkenning
die ongesange
geboorte

Ka' jy hulle vestaan?
Kyk hoe swaar kry ons
dan bring hulle nog
'n kind innie wêreld in,
en sê dis ons happiness
Dit isse gekgeid
ek sê jou!

VI
He' jy al lekkerder geswaai
assie Kaapse draai
he' jy 'n happier
song gesing
of 'n bietere
tong gehoor
en die wyn
o die wyn
he' jy allie
wyn geproe
dis glorie
en halleluja

wie het al gehuil
vir bieter daage
die sout van trane
spoel snot en trane
deur die hiewels
va os liewe
en kyk daar het
'n tuin gegroei
kyk hoe baljaar
die sien van man
innie tuin van trane

heppie! heppie

dissie laaste
Krisana.

SLAVE SONG

Hey have you heard
Majit Omar is singing
at the Grand tonight
alle jiega-lang-jak
'Dina se ding is vim,'
'Daa' kommie Alibama,'
Daarse hoener ommie draai'
en 'Rosa' an' all that sad
slave songs

Wa' wiet jy
vannie slave songs
wa' wiet jy vannie
slawetong?

Ek sing die slawe song
'Ja my baas,
nee my baas,
Jannewarie, Feebewarie, Marts,
April, Mei, June, July.'

Haai moenie hier innie
aisles kom spoegie
jy met jou
skiewe tong.

SONGS

Hey my maat
do you hear the music?
the songs the darkie ous
sing when they grafting

and only if you a
darkie ou
orra bushy ou
you graft like 'at

But we can still sing, hey;
'Wie 't vi' jou gemaak?'
an' all that,
even when the graft
is a shit sweat

Wie 't vi' jou gemaak
sonne oege of 'n tong
Dat jy nog soe
lekker smaak?

HAMURAFIA

Haai sies vi' jou
you think your ous
wurra only grand ous,
the only heroes inna stuk

and your songs
the einste songs
with your big-time jazz
an' your Sarie Marais
(het 'n eier gelê)

Have you ever played
the gomma
the gedoemp of trommels
on oudjaarsaand
of Dollar Brand
orre Slamse jieker
'Hamurafia'?

Sies vi' jou,
Daa' ver,
Jy ken neva-nie

CRIB SONG

O, o, die riete kooi
was die riete kooi
'n lekker nooi
vir my om daarop
te slaap

en die Afrika avontuur
vir Twang Jan Goeweneur
net 'n lekke jol
kaalgat deurie witkop
breukers van Tafelbaai gerol

ennie swaaiende swart keupe
glanster innie middenagmaan
silwer drip-drip
die tuimelende heuwels
van geheime ekstase,
ennie hele history
is opgebogger.

'N BOTTELTJIE WYN, ZOEGA SE DOUGH

I
Karringmelk
en tuisgebakte brood
tamatiesous
en zoega se dough
dis die eenvoudigheid
waaroor jy sing,
jy met jou snaterbek!

En toe os die wyn ondek
het jy gesê die 'heiligheid'
is nou by ons by,
'n borrel Umtas, gebakte brood
en jy,
(luister na my saamgeskraapte gediggies)
'n skraal wind
deur die droege gras.

II
In die verhitte middag
— die son hang lomerig en lui
oor die vaalverbrande velde —
sien ons deur die rooi
van dronkaard-oë
die dans van verleide liefde.

Dans Galiema dans!
voor die wyn
van jou liewe uitloep
soes 'n lugspieëling
in die verte

At last briek jy die silence

(bedomp en stowwerig soes
'n Boekaapse kantien)
'Dis blerry lekker om soe
die tyd deurtebring'.

My oege brand soes warme pee
'Waarom traan jy 'an nou?'
Dissie stilte,
die eeue van stilte.

VERLANGE

Wie' jy warris jou mistake?
dissie dat jy swart issie
of dat jy lulik of dom issie

dis dat jy mens is
mens reuk oener
mens arms
is verheuging vannie
lucky ones
dit remind die gods
dat net hulle
forever liewe

mens reuk
in mens neuste
is maar net 'n invitation
om oek saam te kom lê

moenie worry nie
os is amal
hoere vanne soort

(het jy gehoor van daai god
wie uittie hiemel geskop is
ommat hy oege gemaak het
vi' die Big Boy se girl?)

FREEDOM

Hoe lekke sou
die volkies gelief het
sonne lekke pa
se skreeuery

Met die son
ennie maan
oppie breë velde
dans die kaalgat
seun van man

innie saai van stilte
lê die oes van vrede
lê oener sy eie boem
min gepla met die
wêreld se skulde

Maar wat assie son
ennie maan oener gaan
wie sou dan
innie donke huil?

VLUGTELING

Waar stiek jy nou weg
ou pel, nou dat die son
jou wegstiekplek gevind het?
(wat daarvan as jy
'n Immorality kind is?)

Kyk hoe krap die son
soes 'n honger hond
tussen ie asbakke
van os veliede
en bloeiend, djurre,
kyk hoe skeur hy sy vleis
oppie skerp rotse
van jou memry

The morning bleeds!
hy's sat!
kyk net allie gazies,
djurre ou pellie-broer,
nou het jy die
dag oek vermoor!

(jy me' jou
'My toppie was a
Talianer' storie.)

DIE KLEUR VAN LIEFDE

Ko stiek 'n kers op, liefie,
net een kers is genoeg
om innie half donker
te wys wie os is
en waar os is.

Kyk hoe dans die
donker van os liggaams
op die donker mure,
die vlam bedaar
en staan stokstyf.

Hoe donker is jou oege,
die donker van die aarde.
Hoe rooi die vlam van jou lippe,
die rooi van die Karoo
Hoe dor die dorsheid.

Groot is die vrug van verlange,
ryp soes die kleur van 'n wond,
blaas uit die kers liefie,
in daai laaste oomblik
sien ek die sweet tap,
swart pêrels oor
'n geslote oog.

HALLELUJA

'Halleluja!'
sê die preekvader

dik matte van stilte
wilde reuke in die tent
'n stoel skyf
'n neus blaas

'Save jouself, bekeer,
vir jou siel se sakes'

Jy het high hopes nê
dat die wille water
sal subside
dat die banjo weer stil
in die stille nag sal tril

dat kinderdae se vrede weer
oor die wit en kalm strate
van kinderdae sal heers

'Wies geloewig innie Allemagtig!'
Kyk: die geswerm kom uit
       die donker nag!'
Jurre! dis my dermstukke
op hul geelgroen tanne!

En jy hoep nog
hoep nog God
sal ons velos.
Halleluja.

DIE NUWE ORDER

'Half past twelve. How the hours have passed.
Half past twelve. How the years have passed.'

C.P. Cavafy.

Hoe lank sit os al hier
allien en loemerig
gesus deurie ritmiese
stilte vannie ure,
o hoe jonk was ek
hoe jonk my plesier
nou: 'n vergete lus
'n pyn in my lieste

en daar buite
dans die meide
ennie klonges
o jeugdigheid
is onvervlekte
jagsegeid

hoe lank moet os
hier sit, liefling,
en die koue koester?
dis halfpast twelve
en jou oege raak dof

o die tamboer is nou nog
en die ou hoer is nou nog
maar pellie, daar issie
mee trane nie

watse skolliebees
slinger Jerusalem heen
vir sy geboortenis?

BEGRAFNIS VAN 'N BLOM EN 'N DROEM

I
Die gekkegeid het gekom
met die winde
uitie Karoo
droege asem van
'n korrelkop Cassandra,
die gode het besluit:
Julle tyd is nou hier.

En die saad die vlieg
word versprei deurie land
bevrug en gekweek —
en ek het opgekom,
vol op dié heilige rivier,
en die rivier is op vloed

dit neem lelies
en ander dooie blomme
na hul begrafnis
by die see.

II
Soweto brand vandag,
gie my 'n skyf
van jou sigaret
wat jy soe wegstiek
in jou gloeiende hand,
o liefling, kom loep saam
ek is koud, en soe alleen
kom, die wille water
maak my bang.

III
O man van die aarde
rotte buite die deur
van die hemel, kyk:
ek blom!

nie die blom van koring
of die groen van dowwe
weivelde nie
waar die gode van man
gebore is, nee
dit is die groei
van rots uit robbish

ek sing my song
alleen
innie stilte
vannie hiemels
waar die wind nie
soe vriendelik issie

nog minder is ek
droster van die skys.

IV
Kyk hoe loep die roek
uit jou hanne my bra
Soweto brand,
en jou sigaret is klaar,
wie gaan nou vir ons 'n
roekie gee?
Byt jou lip en kom, broer
na die geselskap van ons soort,
warm is die liggaam
van my medebroer

met sy stink kombers
en sy suster hoer.

V
O man van die skoffel
al die seisoene
wat jy met my liefling
gelê het, in die gras,
vars met die dou van lente

en toe vloek jy haar
vir 'n slegte hoer
toe jy die reuk van
songębrande arms
in haar hare geruik het

nou wandel sy
met die wind
wat teer oor
die land van my hart
wei

en voorberei
vir die komende winter,
jou somer is al weg
en ek, en sy,
sal die wêreld versier.

VI
Ennie winter het gekom
om net 'n nogge winter
te verplaas,
kyk oorie liege horison:
die blare hang soes
trane van die see

ennie vee wei op
swartgebrande gras
by die nagmaal
dans die kersie
oppie tafel,
sad gesigte wat
maar mak sit en sing
daars niks wonderful
van 'n begrafnis nie.

VII
Ou pellie, ou broer,
man met die songebrande arms
ontgrawe die rots
uit die weivelde vannie dood
kyk: daar is vrug oppie boem
en moenie vegiet, gie my 'n skyf
voordat die wêreld afbrand.

VIII
En sing van die
onmakheid van os eeu,
en sing en vegiet
en vegiet en dans
en dans en juig
en drink die wyn
van forgetfulness
A happy nation
het g 'n memry,
of histry nie.

WEDDING

Ek gaan wedding toe.
Julle dink sieker
dis net die vraery
die ietery en
die singery

die wit rok
en die medora
op haar kop;
die tradisies van
'n vreemde volk

Maar wat vannie liefde;
kyk hoe stadig volg
sy oege haar
terwyl sy loep,
en die bloos op haar wang
die herinnering van 'n
druppel swiet op sy lip.

gister, in die koel
van 'n soemerkamer,
(voordat liefde bekragtig was
deur die blindoegprag
van tradisie.)

DAE VAN 1973

Sonstrale op jou gesig
heuningdruppels van swiet
rooi soes die wyn
wat os nie mag drink 'ie.

Dis amper tyd, luister,
die bilal bang
(die Muezzin, soes hulle sê,
roep ons om te bid).

Daar buite stap die
salige mense aan,
skerp, uitgemete stappe
die helderheid vannie geloef
op hul gesigte.

Die gebedsuur
hang soes eeue
op os gedagte,
jy wil nie hê
ek moet aan jou raak nie.

Ver, vaal in die brandende son,
brou Tafelberg die
wolke van 'n storm

dreigement van die gode,
vir ons, son-versotte sondaars,
Adam en Eva
in Hanoverstraat.

PARADYS

O paradys,
koel paradys van Afrika
jou see roer soes
die onrustige wortels
van os liewens

en gie tog nie liewe
aan die droeme
van die mense wat
jy hier vegiet het

hier, om my,
briek hulle my stad af,
Distrik Ses,
hulle sloop jou
klip vir klip
rots van my
geskiedenis

Op die muur van
my laaste herberg
hardloop 'n kokkerotjie
geheimsinnig en stil

'n voortieken van my liewe
liefde en hoep
moet ek in donkergate
wegstiek

Êrens in die skiemerlig
tril 'n banjo, êrens,
op 'n terras toegegroei
met 'n vygie slingerplant

mense sing en mense lag
die menslike gesels van elkedag
o paradys, koel paradys
van Afrika,
watte sad memries skep jy
in die skiemer van ons dae

waarom trek jy
die booie soe vas?

MORE

Slaap liefling
deur hierie
onstuimige uur.

Daar buite val
'n ontydige mis
'n nag vir skollies
en ander vryers
'n doodstillige uur
wanne os te bang is
om te fluister.

Die stilte hang
swaar en ryk
soes miangstokkies
op 'n Donragaand
en die jackhammers
is oek stil, en die
bulldozers het ga slaap,
gie my stad
'n tydelike pouse
(al is sy derms oek
al half uitgetrek)

Ver af in Roosstraat
soes die bus draai
en die mis rol
en alles huistoe jag

in die ou huisies
van os moeders
wag 'n moeder vir jou
die meisie wat more trou

en more kom die jackhammers weer
pik-pik soes kraaie
op die oorskietsels
van os liefde.

GISTER HERROEP

Wat is daar
om te onthou?

Jy ry met die bus
al langs die see
en wys jou seun
die vuil, olierige skepe
wat swoeg en swiet
soes ou dronklappe

en daar . . .
daar in daai ou
afdakhuisie
het ek 'n man geken

'Argus!
Late Final!
Argus mêrrem
Argus!
Squatters Evicted!.'

DIE BERG

O liefling
nou is jy oek weg
al wa oobly
issie leeg-oeg winkels
van Hanoverstraat,
ennie berg.

Die berg wa
die skolliegode
vir die winter hibernate
kyk: hoe oorstroom dit
met die wolk
van hul baljaar.

Al wa oobly
is hierie memry
om optegaar
vi 'n koue
wintersnag.

SHEILA'S DAY

Sy het teen my skouer gelê
die bediener-meisie
half soes 'n seevoël
teen 'n muur gewaai,
en haa rok het stil geval,
soes die kalm slip-slap
vannie see oppie wal,

toe het sy weggegaan
na die Joburg toe
om te werk
en in Doornfontein
'n huis gekry
'n man gekry
'n kind gekry
met oege soe blou
soes die spits vannie see.

MORE HERROEP

Ek loep weer
deur os stad
en sien weer die meisie
innie viswinkel.
Sy issie meer soe jonk nie,
sy issie meer soe mooi nie,
die tyd ennie seisoen
is teen haar

maar sy klou vas
en word grys,
sug en stiek weg
haar trane,
en maak haar rok
ommie bodice soe
net 'n bietjie
stywer vas.

Service met 'n smile:
tien sent se snoek
op laasnag se brood
en daar's 'n blom
in haar boesem,
'n effens glimlag,
glorie vannie nag
se liefde.

DAE VAN 1977
(Winter in Fordsburg)

'Wat kyk jy?
wil jy 'n stuk hê?'

Jou oege gloei
soos dowwe vonke
uitspatsels uit die
koue vuur
van ons droeme.

Jy skat,
my swart vlamink
met die vals
pienk hare,
dans
jou lank slank biene
was die beeld
van my swart
bewustheid.

Nou dans jy
jou ellendige dans
en droem jou leeg-oeg droeme
'n dooie ster wat stamp-stamp
deur die kosmos drif

'Hey meid!
hou op jou sterre
soe teen my skuur.'